ESSAYS
OF A
YOUNG
MELANATED
CHRISTIAN
CONSERVATIVE
Woman

MAGA, Woke, and Concerned.
The Enemy is Not Who You Think it is.

By Dominique Galbraith

ESSAYS OF A YOUNG MELANATED CHRISTIAN CONSERVATIVE WOMAN

DOMINIQUE GALBRAITH

Produced in the United States of America
ISBN: 978-1-7354854-0-9
Uniiqe Life Publishing
NY, NY 10035
www.TheBPLife.net

Dedications

This book is dedicated to my mother, who once woke me up at 3 a.m. to tell me, "Don't limit yourself." Your years of hard work and generosity were not in vain.

This book is dedicated to my three sisters, especially Mia. Soon, you will realize what The Lord has put in you and why He made you the way He did.

This book is dedicated to Hazel and Anthony. Thank you for taking God seriously and inspiring me to go deeper in Him.

And last but not least, this book is dedicated to my love, my husband, Garry. You are truly God-sent.

Table of Contents

Preface: The Author's Heart

I wrote this book in 2020 with one primary goal: to share the revelation God gave me about the true ethnic identity of Black Americans, the root cause of systemic racism, and who their true enemies are.

My heart in this matter is that Black Americans would come into the same truth and freedom that I have experienced, breaking free from the bondage of the racism narrative. After publishing this book and revisiting it three years later, having grown and increased in knowledge, I realized it needed to be edited to reflect my growth and current understanding of what is true concerning race in America. While my core message remains unchanged, the original version of this book carries the sentiments and residue of who I was—someone who still harbored bitterness and resentment toward white people. Although I had come to the truth, my perspective was still tainted by decades of indoctrination and loyalty to the "Black struggle" narrative.

As someone whose heart and efforts are set on bringing people to the truth, the last thing I want to do is reinforce the lies they are being told from an outdated perspective that no longer reflects who I am. My prayer is that both Black and White Americans will see the truth and reject the lies meant to divide us. I pray that the revelation shared in the following chapters concerning Black Americans' ethnic identity as Jews will not be dismissed as anti-Semitism or Hebrew-Israelite rhetoric, but understood for what it truly is: truth shared to bring healing to a broken people and foster unity and support for those in the body of Christ who have long held a love for, and are called to pray for, God's covenant people. For those who find this confounding, I encourage you to pray, testing what I have written by The Holy Spirit.

The Dream and The Revelation

On June 14, 2015, I had the following dream:

I was in a large group of protesters, and we were protesting injustice. We suddenly approached a very important door that gave us access to the White House, but we were in a small waiting area. I wasn't the one leading the protest, but somehow I managed to get everyone's attention and asked, "Are there any believers here?" and "Where are the prayer warriors?" Most of the crowd raised their hands. So I began to tell the crowd that the Bible says we do not wrestle against flesh and blood but against spiritual wickedness in high places and authorities. We have to keep this in mind, as this is the reason why we are seeing the injustices that we face. I was preparing them to enter into spiritual warfare before entering the White House. As I was speaking, some young girls who had just been released from a detention center joined us, trying to disrupt us while pretending to be part of the movement.

I had no recollection of this dream. But on June 14th, 2020, as I was pondering whether or not I should make my political views known amid racial tension and hatred for Trump, this dream, which I had shared in a Facebook post five years ago, popped up on my timeline. Here is the corrected version:

I believe that this dream was God's confirmation for me to speak publicly, exposing evil and deception in politics, especially as it relates to the Black community.

I also wanted people, especially Black Americans, to know who the real enemies are, their strategies to keep us down, and how we overcome evil. That is where this book was born.

It was never my intention to get involved in politics beyond my random rants on Facebook. But the more I researched and the more I prayed, the more passionate I became about informing people of the truth.

It seems as though racial tensions break out during every presidential election cycle, and I don't believe this is a coincidence. But there was something about George Floyd's death that just hit differently. I was grieved, like most people, and consumed by the media as well. The issue of race had no doubt become a national conversation again.

As I was listening to conservative voices share their views on race and make their cases as to why they do not believe racism exists in a form that has a significant impact on Black life, I was not convinced. This is where my culture and my political views clashed. But I learned, as a Christian, not to lean on my own understanding, or anyone else's, but to seek God and find out what He has to say on the matter. I remember one night praying before bed and asking the Lord, "What is the state of Black Americans? What is going on?"

Is institutional racism real?

He began to bring to my memory the many incidents of injustice and mistreatment Black Americans have faced, and still face, in this country. In doing so, He confirmed that yes, institutional racism is real. But He took it a step further.

I went to bed and woke up in pain around 3:00 a.m. I was fighting against passing out and had difficulty breathing. I nudged my husband and asked him to pray for me. I was tempted to go to the emergency room and tried my very best to avoid it. After a few minutes of prayer, everything went away. It was as if nothing had happened. I suddenly felt fine, but I couldn't go back to sleep. I decided to stay up and pray. As I went to the place where I often prayed and talked to God, He answered the question I had asked before going to bed: What is the state of Black America, and why are these things happening?

God's word to me was that they (Black Americans) are JEWS. Suddenly, everything made sense.

He said many of the issues they face are due to this lost identity. When people don't know who they are, they are vulnerable to abuse by others and abuse themselves. As God revealed this to me, I began to think about the Old Testament accounts of the children of Israel and the judgment they faced when they rejected God. But I was also reminded of His mercy and faithfulness to them.

This was also a reminder that this battle is spiritual. Anyone who has studied scripture knows the trials the Children of Israel endured when they lost their way.

The Jews have always faced persecution from the time God chose them as a nation and made a covenant with them. When you read the biblical accounts of the Hebrews in Egypt and how Pharaoh (the descendants of Ham) oppressed the children of Israel (the descendants of Shem) or of their captivity in Babylon, there are many similarities in struggles, mindset, and resilience.

Though our ethnicity cannot save us, God has not forsaken the children of Israel. I believe that God's heart is to reveal the true ethnicity of Black Americans as part of His plan to restore, heal, and bring about justice that is not void of righteousness. He wants to open their eyes to recognize that Jesus is their Savior, whom many of His people have rejected because He was introduced to them by those oppressing them. I believe that God is calling His chosen people, Israel, back to His way of life and wants us to know who the real enemies are and learn to hear and be led by His voice.

Chapter One:

Restoration of The Black Jews

To my Black American brothers and sisters brought to this strange land, you who have been disconnected from your true ethnic identity: A people who don't know who they are or their origins are destined to suffer oppression and confusion. You have experienced battles both physically and spiritually and have long asked the question, 'Why?' You have lost the principles of your forefathers and have been manipulated into upholding values and beliefs that were not only destructive but were never yours.

You are not attacked because you are the least; you are attacked because you're chosen.

Your day of reckoning has come.

You are a Jew. You are of the tribe of Judah, a Hebrew by ethnicity. You are a member of God's chosen people, Israel, a descendant of Shem, Abraham, Isaac, and Jacob. Your God made a promise to them, and that promise is available to you. **If only you knew your power.**

You are a Jew. Your God has always provided for you. He poured out His blessings and displayed His power through your ancestors, and every nation feared you because of your God. **If only you knew your power.**

You are a Jew. You have historically overcome adversity by the supernatural power of God. While other nations trusted in their kings and false gods, you trusted and called upon the name 'Yahweh,' The Great I Am. **If only you knew your power.**

You are a Jew. But despite being chosen above all other nations, despite God making a covenant with you, and despite Him delivering you time and time again, you turned from Him. You called upon your ancestors and participated in witchcraft. You followed after the gods of other nations. **You surrendered your power.**

You are a Jew. He warned us that He would send us in ships to a strange land and that we would be slaves again. He warned us that we would be scattered among the nations. We failed to heed His warning. **You surrendered your power.**

You are a Jew. You were enslaved in a strange land—raped, abused, experimented upon, forced into hard labor, and then given some form of freedom. You went from physical chains to mental ones. **If only you knew your power.**

You are a Jew. In God's sovereignty and mercy, you were reintroduced to your Messiah, Jesus, in this strange land. **You were reintroduced to your power.**

You are a Jew. Even amid your oppression, abuse, and neglect, you called upon Jesus' name, and God blessed you. You built churches to worship Him, thriving towns, bought land and property, started businesses, and created inventions. Amid your oppression, **you exercised your power.**

You are a Jew. Your enemy saw you prospering and thriving. Your power became a threat. Nevertheless, you kept building, and you sang. You created a new culture. You shaped and transformed every form of entertainment, even as an oppressed people. You impacted, and continue to impact, the world with your culture. **If only you knew your power.**

You are a Jew. Your adversary convinced you that your help needed to come from the government. You allowed the adversary to shift your focus and values from building and owning your own, to mandated integration. **You stopped trusting in your power.**

You are a Jew. You let your guard down. You embraced media that gave you a new identity, one you did not collectively choose, but one your brethren sold out to sell you. They gave you abortion clinics, drugs, and welfare in exchange for your patriarchs and future generations. **Where is our power?**

You are a Jew. Surviving, fighting, and destroying your brother. They sold you a distorted vision of this strange land's 'Dream.' They used the media to convince you to embrace the very things that would destroy you as a people group. **If only you knew your power.**

You are a Jew. Through it all, many of you took hold of your destiny and fought. You turned back to God, realized your dreams, and began to use the tools made available to you. You created businesses, built strong families, and bought property, all in this strange land. **You reclaimed your power.**

Your battle in this nation is not merely natural but spiritual. Israel has been hated throughout history. The Bible tells your history and leads you to hope and answers for the ills you face from within and without. The Lord says, *'If my people, who are called by my name, will humble themselves and pray and seek my face and turn from their wicked ways, then I will hear from heaven, and I will forgive their sin and will heal their land.'* - 2 Chronicles 7:14

Reclaim your inheritance. Abandon those things that destroy you, including bitterness and hatred. **Walk in your power.**

I share this revelation about your ethnic identity not so that you would begin to live according to the Old Covenant laws nor as a mandate to adopt Jewish customs and traditions.

Our ethnicity, even that of being a chosen people, cannot save us. Our Messiah is Jesus, and it is in His name alone that we are saved from our sin and escape the judgment of Hell. In Him, you are safe. In Him, you are valid. In Him, your life matters. In Him, you will find healing from your anger and resentment towards your brothers and sisters who may seem like your enemies but have the heart of our Savior. In Him, we have power. **In Jesus, you have overcome.**

Chapter Two:

To My White Brothers and Sisters In Christ

I want to begin this letter by sharing an experience that God brought to my mind during the protests and riots that followed George Floyd's death. At first, I watched the protests in solidarity, but that quickly turned to disgust as I witnessed the riots. However, God allowed me to see things from a different perspective—to look beyond the obvious and view the deeper issue from His perspective. He reminded me of an experience I had, which I'd like to share.

I frequently took my eldest son to Toddler Storytime at the local library. It was usually an enjoyable time of storytelling, singing, and dancing with other mothers and their children. Afterward, the librarian would bring out toys for the kids to share and play with.

On this particular day, one child repeatedly took away whatever toy my son decided to play with. I stood there—something I regret now—hoping the child's parents would step in and stop him. I didn't want to be aggressive with someone else's child, and I thought, "It's just toys; my son will get over it."

But when playtime ended and the toys were put away, Elijah had a meltdown. As I stood there, a mix of emotions overwhelmed me. I felt helpless because nothing I did could console him. I felt tremendous guilt because I could have intervened, but I didn't. Now, everyone had to witness the wrath of a child who felt robbed of justice.

Elijah felt as though he had been unfairly deprived of what others around him had freely enjoyed. The person who could have done something—me, his mother—stood by and did nothing.

For some, the riots that followed George Floyd's death were an opportunity for exploitation. But for many in the Black community, these riots were an emotional response to a very real injustice. The nation was witnessing the wrath of people who had grown weary of mistreatment. Unfortunately, these actions played right into the hands of those responsible for that mistreatment.

In my story, my son represents the Black American community that has been reduced to being treated like helpless children, mistreated—patronized and brainwashed by the education system, media, and entertainment industry into accepting an identity of oppressed and debaucherous. Leftists, who embrace communist ideals and work primarily through the Democratic Party, have systematically worked to destroy the Black community both psychologically and economically. These efforts keep the Black community dependent on them as their so-called institutional savior.

It's no secret that Black Americans overwhelmingly vote Democrat, believing the party is "for the people," despite the failures and devastation in many predominantly Black neighborhoods under Democratic leadership. A key strategy in their effort to maintain power is stirring up and exploiting racial tension. They cast blame on White Americans for all of Black Americans' problems, painting them as the bourgeoisie in their Marxist narrative. This tactic increases division between Black and White Americans and diverts attention away from the Black community economically empowering itself through traditional means. The ultimate goal is to destabilize the nation and steer it toward communism.

Manning Johnson, a high-ranking member of the Communist Party during the 1930s who later accepted Jesus Christ and left the party, warned about this in his book "Color, Communism, and Common Sense". He wrote:

"Little did I realize, until I was deeply enmeshed in the red conspiracy, that just and seeming grievances are exploited to transform idealism into a cold, ruthless weapon against the capitalist system—that this is the end toward which all communist efforts among the Negroes are directed."

Johnson detailed how an international coalition of communists infiltrated government, institutions, media, and churches, aiming to destroy the moral and constitutional foundation of America in order to overthrow it. He explained how Black Americans were being used as pawns in this agenda.

Johnson also pointed out that communists not only stirred up racial tensions but also actively sabotaged economic growth in Black communities. He mentioned how Black neighborhoods were labeled "ghettos" to dissuade Black Americans from building and investing in their communities in the same way other ethnic groups have done. He also provided an example of how plans to build a Black-owned hospital in Harlem to serve the Black community were derailed by communists.

While the Jim Crow era may be over, efforts to economically suppress the Black community persist today. Modern-day tactics, such as labeling math "racist" to justify lowering educational standards for Black students, are examples of policies that leave Black children undereducated and unable to compete in the job market. This increases the likelihood of criminal activity and dependence on the state.

Black men, in particular, have been sold out to the private prison industry, often receiving excessive sentences for non-violent offenses, which further destroys Black families. Meanwhile, the justice system in Democrat-run cities has swung to the other extreme, allowing repeat offenders to be released back into communities to cause further destruction. Additionally, Black homeowners in gentrifying neighborhoods are often harassed by developers or pressured to sell their homes while simultaneously being hit with drastic property tax increases and the dissolution of public transportation lines, adding further pressure to move.

These are just a few modern examples of how the communist left hinders economic growth in Black communities. While overtly racist policies are less common today, socialist policies in many Democrat-run cities have the greatest impact on Black citizens due to their socioeconomic status and culture. These issues, combined with the long history of eugenics, the targeting of Black communities by Planned Parenthood for abortions, and the promotion of the dangerous COVID-19 vaccine under the guise of "medical justice," reveal a broader agenda. Bill Gates, a known leftist with eugenicist ties, for example, infamously suggested that Black people should be prioritized for the vaccine—a statement that carried racist undertones, suggesting that race made one more vulnerable.

Though the end goal of this mass indoctrination, economic suppression, and exploitation of racial bitterness is to establish a new political and economic system, it is still state-sponsored racism. The riots were stoked by forces outside the Black community to push an agenda that had nothing to do with justice or advancing Black interests. Sadly, many within these protests were Black people who had experienced injustice without knowledge of the hidden agenda and without understanding who their true enemy was.

This is not to excuse rioting or absolve the Black community of responsibility. Neither is it to place the issues of Black Americans solely on the shoulders of external forces. But as God revealed, the enemy's plan was not only to destroy the Black community using outside forces but also to manipulate the community into self-destruction.

I share this story in the hope of opening your eyes to an overlooked truth and calling for compassion. I hope it leads you to pray and intercede for Black Americans. As the ecclesia, the spiritual thermostat of the nation, we must look beyond the surface and address the root causes, principalities, and forces at play—when it comes to social injustice and what is perceived as such. Only by recognizing these deeper issues can we begin to heal our nation's divide and expose our common enemy.

Chapter Three:

To My Black Brothers and Sisters In Christ

The Black Church, birthed out of your love for God, a desire to gather and worship, and the rejection you faced from your white brethren, exists as a safe space to freely worship God in your cultural expression. You have been a pillar, a place of refuge, hope, healing, deliverance, a breeding ground for talent, and the birthplace of God-given purpose for millions. In your weakness, in the face of discrimination, God has been with you.

I have struggled for years with anger towards those in the white evangelical movement and what seemed like their disregard for the issues concerning the Black community. I've questioned and judged whether or not they are truly Christians and harbored resentment towards them, especially during election seasons when racial tensions seem to be the highest. However, God exposed this sin within me and how I allowed lies from the media to cause me to resent our white brothers and sisters. We are still the body of Christ and will all have to give an account one day for our actions.

My concern is that the culture we've created in the land of our oppression has become an idol. We share the hurt of those of our race who are not saved, but we are called to have a different response. In our failure to heal from the afflictions of this nation, we have made decisions from a place of resentment and idolatry. We have prioritized our culture over the Kingdom in our advocacy and political affiliations.

The worship of the idol of "Blackness" (our cultural and racial identity) has resulted in us politically aligning with politicians who approve of and create policies that conflict with God's word and His ways. We are deceived by their promises to our people and communities. Not only have we allowed them into our pulpits, but we have also allowed them to use us for political gain, all while they fail to keep the promises they've made. We are supporting politicians who will sign laws into effect that will bring about the persecution of the church. This support and alliance have been part of our method in fighting for "justice" as Black people but will come at the expense of our liberty to preach the full gospel truth as Christians and exercise our faith freely.

Have we exchanged our commission to advance the Kingdom for the mission of Black power? We've promoted their propaganda to our people and have helped perpetuate the victim mentality instead of telling our people that the gospel gives power to the people. It is Jesus who makes us free and gives us wisdom in using our gifts and abilities to create economic freedom for our families and communities. We have been so focused on Washington and what it is or isn't doing that we have failed our communities. We should be convicted by the fact that people in need sit in our churches on Sunday and have to look to the government on Monday. We should be convicted by the fact that we say and quote, "Greater is He that is within me than he that is in the world," but have not dealt with the spiritual warfare in our neighborhoods. Our communities are filled with churches that have not walked in the power they claim to have.

We were positioned to be the answer. This is not to say that we should not be concerned with politics or involved in the process of choosing the leaders of the land, but the resentment we are harboring has blinded us to the bigger battles around us and caused us to view everything through the skewed lens of race. We have even gone so far as to abandon the topics of abortion and sexual preference out of fear of offending others because it is politically incorrect to do so according to those we have politically aligned ourselves with.

This is not a call for the Black Church to abandon its pursuit of justice, but it cannot be absent of righteousness. This is a call for the Black Church to prayerfully examine how we go about this pursuit and what political and social allegiances we have made to bring about the results we desire. We are Christians before we are Black. It is our faith in Jesus that ought to dictate our decisions, not our cultural or racial identity. This means any aspect of our culture that is inconsistent with the

Word and standards of God must be laid down. If not, we have made it an idol.

"They worship me in vain; they teach as doctrine the precepts of men. You have disregarded the commandment of God to keep the tradition of men." He went on to say, "You neatly set aside the commandment of God to maintain your own tradition" (Mark 7:7).

Let us repent. Let us put our trust in God to give us a strategy to fight this battle. Let us turn from the racist ways that we have both normalized and justified. Let us heal so that we no longer view everything through the lens of race and miss the bigger picture. Let us heal so that we can engage with our White brothers and sisters of the faith in healthy ways, so we are not easily offended. Let us bury our resentment so that we can collectively operate as the Kingdom.

"Let all bitterness and wrath and anger and clamor and slander be put away from you, along with all malice" (Ephesians 4:31).

Chapter Four:

Abortion:
Genocide of Our Prophets

In the book of Exodus, while the children of Israel lived in Egypt, Pharaoh's response was:

"Look," he said to his people, "The Israelites have become too numerous and too powerful for us." (Exodus 1:10)

So what did Pharaoh do? He oppressed the people he felt threatened by and ordered their sons to be murdered at birth.

Pharaoh represents oppressive leadership in government that worked in opposition to the children of God. Egypt, in some contexts of scripture, is used to represent a place of spiritual bondage. Pharaoh's tactics are far more sophisticated these days, but the goal remains the same. What we now have come to accept as "reproductive rights," aka abortion in America, is one of the ways in which modern-day Pharaohs, who seek to oppress and eliminate the Jews (Black Americans), carry out their plans.

In the years following the release of Black Americans from slavery, despite harsh treatment and Jim Crow policies, Black Americans had unified families, were growing in numbers, and were building strong communities like Black Wall Street.

Amid their display of resilience, a plan to control and eliminate Black Americans was in the works. Planned Parenthood, the nation's largest provider of abortions, formerly known as The American Birth Control League, was the brainchild of a eugenicist, Margaret Sanger. Her idea of "birth control" was to eliminate the "undesirable," the poor, and the feeble-minded through "science"—all of which were characteristics attributed to Black people in the early 1900s, especially among liberal intellectuals.

At the time this book was written, Planned Parenthood was subsidized by the United States government and received over $300 million in funding. Over 70% of their clinics are located in or near Black and minority neighborhoods, and 40% of their abortions are performed on Black women.

The topic of abortion is a sensitive one for the Black community. Many uphold the belief that it is a woman's choice. Some are indifferent, while others believe it is murder and should be illegal—or at the very least, that tax dollars should not be used to fund abortions. What most don't realize is that abortion in America—and in various African nations, where it is forced upon leaders in the form of "aid"—is part of an agenda to depopulate African nations and eliminate and oppress Black Americans. The belief in "reproductive rights" or the right to choose is the result of a highly successful marketing campaign that conveniently fails to mention that the body parts of unborn, aborted babies are sold for various uses. It also neglects to highlight that the largest provider of abortion was started by a known racist and eugenicist.

Some will argue that while this may have been the original plan, it has changed. That is hard to believe when, even today, the vast majority of aborted babies are people of color, and the Black population in America has not grown.

My concern is that our collective struggles as a group, and our individual struggles in this nation, have caused us to be so focused on surviving that we overlook the bigger battles being waged against us in various forms. My concern is that when we rise up to fight against injustice, we are playing checkers with a devil who is playing chess. We have tuned out to the fact that abortion is the number one killer of Black lives, often due to convenience.

Most tribes, nations, and people groups throughout history understood that if they wanted their culture and name to carry on, and if they wanted to increase their power in decision-making, they did so by being fruitful and multiplying. It is unfortunate that the Black community has come to accept many things that are contrary to the flourishing of a people group. Many have questioned how it can be an attack or agenda against the Black population when no one is forcing women to abort their children. "It is their choice!" they say.

My response to that is similar to how you point to racism or white supremacy whenever the issue of crime in our community is brought up. When Black man A kills Black man B, we often say that this was a choice resulting from oppression that began years ago and has modern-day implications on the decisions Black men make today. We have developed a tendency to point out oppression when it fits our narrative.

I am among those who believe that an unborn child is a human being and, though he or she is in a woman's body, is not part of the woman's body. The child has its own heartbeat and DNA. I believe abortion is murder. Many don't agree with that, but I have to ask: Why is a person charged with double homicide when they murder a pregnant woman? Some lawmakers have changed this to justify their approval of late-term abortion. Why are women who are obviously pregnant judged for not taking care of their bodies, which are housing a baby, if they don't uphold societal standards? Does the baby become less human and no longer worthy of life only when the mother decides to abort?

For many years, I was indifferent, until my Christian values began to clash with what I was conditioned to believe growing up in New York. As I've grown as a woman and a Christian, I have come to believe that not only is abortion wrong, but it is part of an agenda that disproportionately targets "the poor," which in many circles is code for Black people.

This agenda became even clearer to me when I became pregnant with my first child. I discovered that it goes beyond just one company performing abortions—it is systematic. There are places in this country that have decided to actively and invasively control the "family planning" of low-income families through public healthcare.

When I suspected I might be pregnant, I looked up a free clinic to take a pregnancy test since I had no health insurance and had been paying for my visits out of pocket. When I took the test and the nurse gave me the results, I was elated. The nurse, barely looking me in the face, asked, "Oh, you're happy?" I was confused. Didn't she know that children are a blessing? Perhaps she didn't realize this was my first pregnancy, or maybe she had seen so many women come through the clinic who weren't excited about their pregnancies. I may never know the answer, but I do know that life is precious regardless of the circumstances, and for some reason, it seems everyone is losing sight of that.

A week or two later, I received a Benefits card I hadn't applied for from the state. I called the number provided because I didn't know what the "benefits" were and wanted to inquire. The benefit being offered to me, a 30-year-old, newly married, and newly pregnant woman, was sterilization. Who gave the state the right to prescribe sterilization to me? My socioeconomic status and my race did.

"It now remains for the United States government to set a sensible example to the world by offering a bonus or a yearly pension to all obviously unfit parents who allow them to be sterilized by harmless and scientific means. In this way, the moron and the diseased would have no posterity to inherit their unhappy condition. The number of the feebleminded would decrease and a heavy burden would be lifted from the shoulders of the fit." -Margaret Sanger, "The Function of Sterilization," Oct 1926.

Source:
https://www.nyu.edu/projects/sanger/webedition/app/docu ments/show.php?sangerDoc=304387.xml

As we can see, Margaret Sanger's suggestions have been implemented to some degree in our government. Reflecting on my prenatal care and mandatory visits, I find it odd that the same system that required me to adhere to their rules and regulations for my unborn child was the same system that promoted and supported "my right to choose" abortion.

I remember being in the hospital when it was time to give birth. During the three days I was there, one doctor was persistent in asking if I wanted birth control. She asked me at least three times. The third time she asked, I gave a stern response and demanded that she not return to ask a fourth time. At that moment, when I told her not to come back to my room to push her drugs on me again, I felt like I was finally taking control. What made her fail to consider that my husband and I might want to have children consecutively? Our socioeconomic status did, and I don't doubt that race played a factor. Did she assume what my family plan was, or was she imposing her idea of what my family plan should be? I had three seemingly racist experiences (all at different places within NYC) during my first pregnancy as a young woman. Each experience was an effort to control how, when, or if I reproduced. None took into consideration my family plan before attempting to push their plan on my family. They didn't care.

There is a reason why NYC is the abortion capital of America, and it goes beyond the fact that some women choose to abort their children. Black life seems to be expendable, including those in the womb.

"We who advocate Birth Control, on the other hand, lay all our emphasis upon stopping not only the reproduction of the unfit but upon stopping all reproduction when there are no economic means of providing proper care for those who were born in health." - Margaret Sanger, "Birth Control and Racial Betterment" (February 1919).

It's troubling that my community fails to recognize the attack on our future generations through abortion. We've been tricked into sacrificing our future under the guise of "healthcare." Whose rights are we fighting for if more Black babies are being aborted than born in places like New York and 40% of abortions are committed by Black women?

I don't want to seem insensitive to the fact that many women are not getting abortions because they don't care. I am well aware that many do it out of fear and what they believe is in the child's best interest because of their current living situation or because of a father who has no plans of being involved. I won't pretend that I don't wrestle with this issue and understand why someone would choose the route of abortion. However, I am compelled to speak up for the unborn because of my faith regardless of what seems logical. I also know many women who, despite facing the same odds, have decided to keep their children and are grateful that they did.

I know many women who have not been held back by having a child at a difficult time but have been motivated to fight for their dreams and have seen them manifest. I firmly believe that if God allows you to conceive, He can also make a way for you to survive and thrive. If you are considering an abortion and feel that you cannot make it because of your circumstances, you can. I would encourage you, if you are pregnant and considering an abortion, to please reconsider. That child is a blessing regardless of the circumstances, and if God allows that child to be conceived, He will also make a way for you and your child.

I have not had an abortion, but I know what it's like to feel that children will get in the way of your dreams. I know firsthand that God makes a way. Our community needs to reexamine how we view abortion and its impact on our community, as well as take active control over our family planning. Let us promote preventative measures so that abortion doesn't have to be an option, including abstinence and normalizing having children within wedlock in our culture. Let us form support groups and organizations to help women who become pregnant and have no support.

Let us vote for and support politicians who lower taxes and create policies that promote capitalism in ways that encourage small business and entrepreneurship (the surest way out of poverty), instead of focusing on social programs that make it difficult to no longer depend on the system. We need to find ways to prevent the system from making decisions concerning the health of those living in low-income communities.

"Free" is the new slavery. We went from physical slavery to Jim Crow to "free" government assistance. But this "free" comes at the cost of our patriarchs, control over our family planning and decisions concerning our health, the direction of our communities, our freedom to pursue our God-given dreams and our dignity. On a spiritual note: Let the prophets come forth! Let our young kings and queens be born in Jesus' name.

Chapter Five:

I've Got Questions

- Why have we allowed liberals to convince us to hate capitalism and the companies many of them invest in? Why do we vote for socialist/communist leaders when so many of us are creating generational wealth through capitalism?

- Why have we become so trusting of the same media that has misrepresented us, perpetuated stereotypes, and highlighted the worst aspects of our culture for decades?

- Why have we allowed liberals to convince us that animals are to be valued at the same level as humans yet dehumanize our unborn children?

- Why have democratic leaders failed to implement programs like financial literacy, cut home economics, and the arts but prioritize teaching our children about sex and confusing them about gender?

- Why can't we confront injustice AND accountability within the Black community? Why are we suppressing the voice of correction that leads to self-improvement and advancement?

- I remember when Jay-Z said change clothes. I saw black men go from tee-shirts to button-ups. I remember when

Eve started wearing cornrows straight back, and every young black girl followed suit. I remember skateboard culture becoming a thing in the black community because it became a thing in hip-hop. The impact and influence of hip-hop culture are undeniable. Why have we been in denial about the effects that violence and drug use in our music have on our youth?

- How can you blame someone who has been in power for 4 years for problems that have existed for decades and believe that the career politician is the better choice? What has happened in the Black community during Trump's presidency that is unique to your experience in this nation?

- Since we are tearing down statues and canceling things that reinforce white supremacy, why haven't we torn down the Hollywood sign? The symbol that represents an industry that has created and reinforced negative stereotypes, promoted and reinforced colorism and black inferiority? How about we stop supporting artists and the record companies that create, invest in, and promote death and sensuality in culture through music?

- Since we are canceling everything that has a racist history, why haven't we canceled Planned Parenthood?

- Why have we pledged allegiance to a political party that has run our cities for decades with no change except gentrification? If our problem is the system, why do we keep voting for the same people who run the systems that impact us most?

- To my fellow conservatives, How can you deny that institutional racism exists but point out, write books, and highlight the racism in the Democratic party?

Chapter Six:

Trump isn't Your Enemy

Why I support Donald Trump for President

From the beginning of his candidacy, I could never have imagined myself being a Trump supporter. The sight of him made me angry. His supporters made my blood boil. I just couldn't understand how anyone could support him, especially Christians. I watched my trusted sources of local and cable news every day. They painted a picture that I never thought to question. But that changed during the New York State gubernatorial elections. There we were, in the middle of a major election for our state, and my trusted media source chose only to talk about and highlight the Democratic candidate. I barely knew the name of the Republican candidate running against him. To me, it became clear that not only was this media outlet biased, but they were also using their major platform to steer the election in the way they wanted it to go. While I believe that every citizen must research who their officials are and what they stand for, I also believe that the media has the responsibility to report the truth without bias and allow people to think for themselves. How naive of me. This, I have learned, is almost non-existent.

So I started to question, am I getting the full truth about Trump? Have I ever taken the time to understand why some of my brothers and sisters in Christ support Trump? Have I even prayed about it, or was I just leaning on my own understanding? This is what changed everything. Before this, I had no idea what Trump was actually about or his purpose because the media and the people I listened to had me viewing him from a skewed, agenda-led perspective. Being a Black woman, I took the bait and viewed everything through the lens of my identity as a Black person. But Trump, despite his reckless and tasteless tweets and bravado, is standing in the way of something that is an even bigger threat to me as a Hebrew woman and as a Christian. Trump is standing in opposition to globalism/New World Order, or what the church calls the Antichrist agenda.

"Why do the nations rage and the peoples plot in vain? The kings of the earth take their stand and the rulers gather together, against the LORD and against His Anointed One" Psalms 2:1-2

The nations and their kings have always worked in opposition to Jesus, the children of Israel, and The Church. But God has the final victory.

Have you noticed an increase in disdain for Christians, especially in college classrooms? Are you aware of China's persecution of Christians and the communist regime, and how the media supported China as Trump stood up against them?

Look at which party was trying to introduce the digital dollar, the precursor to a one-world currency so that they could make it "easier" for you to get your "free money" during the pandemic. The Democrats. Notice how the Black community was impacted the worst during this pandemic? Notice how churches were deemed non-essential and targeted even when they adhered to CDC regulations. It's a conspiracy for sure, and the powers that be, who work for Satan want you to believe it's all theory. Trump was the outsider who was never expected to win and was not part of their plan. Have you ever seen a President hated this much?

This agenda is about control of wealth and its redistribution (socialism aka communism) that works conveniently in their favor, surveillance, and control of human activity, depopulation, and removing boundaries as it relates to sexual relations, including pedophilia. Sounds crazy? Why are the "experts" suddenly "discovering" that masturbation should be taught to toddlers? Their "scientific" reason is that this helps children to self-regulate their behavior. Why have respected platforms like *The New York Times* written articles about pedophilia not being a crime but a disorder? This is how Satan works through people and organizations to desensitize and condition the masses to accept wickedness and evil as "normal". It will come to a point where if you speak out against such things, you are standing in the way of someone's "happiness" and are being judgmental.

Their war on capitalism and push for globalized free trade is cause for concern, as communism and free trade have historically brought down nations. This is the goal: to destroy the economies of nations, creating a need for a one-world currency. This one-world currency is what the Bible calls the mark of the beast, which everyone must have to buy or sell. We are being brainwashed into hating America and destroying everything about it because we don't like some of its problems. Despite its evils, there are very few places where a person can go from being homeless to being a millionaire through honest living. Are people risking their lives to come here and abandoning all they have for no reason? Have we forgotten that many of you have ancestors who fought and died to secure rights here?

While the Bible is clear that these things must come, one of the ways Satan works is to try to disrupt the timing of what God says will come to pass. This is something that God made clear to me as I decided to stop assuming that I know and instead listen and seek Him on what He had to say. We are being shown grace in this season and are being given the opportunity to get right with God and reintroduce Jesus and His ways back into our culture. The Spirit of God revealed that antichrist policies will come through the Democratic Party and that the majority of media outlets are being used to manipulate and mentally condition people to accept the antichrist when he appears. This is why most of them don't simply present information to you without first twisting it, and then telling you what to think about what was presented.

Most people, when asked why they don't like Trump, will respond by saying he's a bigot, xenophobe, homophobe, or rapist. Very few can list at least one of his policies or clearly articulate what he represents or his party's political ideology. I know I couldn't, and that became very clear once I began to research deeper than what mainstream media had to say. This is not to demonize those who vote Democrat, especially since I was once a Democrat voter. But many of us either don't know the truth, vote primarily out of tradition, or because the media has put the face of white supremacy on the Republican Party and conservatism. Interestingly, many Black Americans have conservative values but don't vote according to those values or celebrate them in popular culture. The same popular culture is run by Democrats.

For me, this coming election is all about policy and supporting a political direction that I believe is best for our country. Neither candidate is perfect. My support for Donald Trump is not based on believing that he is saved or God's gift to Christianity. But I do believe that God is using him. It's interesting how many people can believe that God can use anybody, yet we find ourselves being hostile to the people He chooses because they don't fit our idea of a person God should use. The Bible says He (God) uses the foolish things of this world to confound the wise. I am not calling President Trump a fool (although I've called him worse in the past), but I am saying that God uses methods, images, and people that don't align with what most people would choose.

Many have questioned why I, as a Black woman, would ever vote for a "racist." "He doesn't care about our people!" I've also seen people blaming him for issues that existed well before his 4-year stint in politics. If we continue to make all of our decisions through the lens of race that the communists have created, we will always lose the bigger battle and continue to be blinded to the real racists who are in power and those who want power.

The real racists are the candidates who advocate for Planned Parenthood, an organization started by eugenicist Margaret Sanger, whose plan for "Birth Control and Racial Betterment" was to reduce or eliminate the feeble-minded, the poor, and the "subnormal." With 70% of her Planned Parenthood clinics in Black and minority neighborhoods, it's obvious who she was targeting. The real racists are the ones who support Bill Gates (once considered a possible running mate for Hillary Clinton) and his push for vaccines as a solution for climate change and public "health." Why do you think he believed Black people should be vaccinated first? Why did he and his wife support illegal abortion in Africa? Why has his vaccine come under fire for sterilizing the people in Africa it was supposed to help? Bill Gates has been very forthcoming about his ideas for population control, and for some reason, his target seems to be Black people. I wonder if he got his idea from his father, Bill Gates Sr., who at one point was the head of Planned Parenthood. Democrats have been leading predominantly Black cities for a long time with no results. If it's the system that we have a problem with as Black people, why do we keep voting for the party that has been running the systems that control our communities for decades?

Who are the real racists? As for me, I am done with the party of welfare traps, high taxes, terrible schools, poorly managed budgets, and the facade of "solidarity."

What are Trump's policies and beliefs that positively impact the Black community and Americans in general?

School Choice

School choice is a policy that allows federal dollars to be spent on sending children to the school of their parent's choice, rather than having only their local public school as their only option. Democrats are not only in favor of public schools as the only option backed by federal dollars but have no plan to improve them. Biden wants to do away with charter schools, which year after year have outperformed public schools in places like New York City and are often the only free alternative for low-income communities.

Interestingly, Democrats fight for the right of a woman to choose abortion and for it to be federally funded, but they are against parents being able to access federal funding to choose the school of their choice.

Support of the Second Amendment

Why should we not have the right to bear arms? I am certainly not in agreement with doing away with guns while the people who want to take them have armed security. Guns are still available in places with the strictest gun laws and, coincidentally, the highest crime rates. And yes, self-defense is biblical.

The First Step Act

This executive order has led to the release of over 7,000 inmates, the overwhelming majority of whom are Black. This act also provided funding for rehabilitation programs, education and employment, and occupational training programs, as well as money for a Pell Grant pilot program for the formerly incarcerated.

Transformation of the Federal Jobs Hiring Process Removing College Degree Requirement

"Unnecessary degree requirements exclude otherwise qualified Americans from federal employment, impose the expense of college on prospective workers, and disproportionately harm low-income Americans. The order implements best practices already adopted by private sector leaders to promote equity and inclusion." – Taken from the White House website in 2020.

Opportunity Zones

This executive order provides tax incentives for investment in economically distressed communities. This order has a two-fold benefit: one being more jobs and the revitalization of inner cities, and the other being tax benefits that work in our favor as many of us have become involved in real estate and entrepreneurship. There is one thing that many rich and middle-class families understand, and that is how to pay fewer taxes and legally work the system to their benefit. Many in the Black community either never learned about taxes or failed to extend their knowledge beyond excitement over a yearly tax refund.

Religious Freedom

The Trump administration has been very vocal and active in its support of the church. Trump has worked to support religious freedom and stood for the Church, as well as other religious groups when our local representatives deemed them non-essential. Many say that he is just pandering to his base, but who are we to judge a man's intentions? Are we to be concerned with the reason or the results?

Pro-life Stance

President Trump is the first president to attend a pro-life rally. He has been a vocal advocate against abortion and has worked to defund the largest abortion clinic in America. Our community has long come to believe that abortion is a woman's right to choose, through an effective campaign that has led us to believe that a fetus is not a human being and that this empowers women. What we didn't realize is that this is really an attack on our community's population, started by racist eugenicists. If you are a real racist, it would take more than pro-life voters to get you to fight against the most effective weapon used against the people you hate.

Smaller Government and Deregulation

We have been taught that government oversight and regulation are necessary to constrain big business and "protect" citizens. This is true in some cases. But in other many cases, these policies hurt and stifle businesses of all sizes, often resulting in larger businesses exporting jobs and smaller businesses facing unnecessary regulations and obstacles that make it difficult to advance and build a competitive business. Instead of seeing capitalism as a threat, we ought to recognize it for what it is and take advantage of the opportunities it provides within a capitalist economy. Free enterprise, or capitalism, is the tool that has helped many of our people carve a path using our God-given talents when we had nowhere to turn. I started making the most money I'd ever seen as a teenager when I started my fashion business in my bedroom. At the same time, I was trying to find a job, and no one would hire me. I used the tools I had, the bit of knowledge that I had, and by faith, started a business. There is absolutely no reason for any Black person to vote for or support any politician who is in opposition to capitalism and creates policies that increase taxes and make it difficult for businesses to flourish. Capitalism is one of the ways in which we are able to take control.

We never needed the government to make a way for us. We needed the government to move out of the way for us. We need fair treatment and the conditions that are necessary to pursue our God-given purpose. Why do we believe that the government should play such a huge role in our lives when they have proven on so many occasions that they are not able to do this well nor can they be trusted?

"My thing is that I don't give no person that much power over my path that I'm walking. Not one person can make or break what I'm doing, except me or God." - Nipsey Hussle

I am not advocating for the complete removal of social programs, but there is a clear need for reform and changes within our community so that we no longer rely on the government and fall into the trap of dependency on assistance. In many major cities across America, the cost of living is so high that people cannot afford to live independently of public assistance.

For far too long, we have looked to a two-party system for answers. On the one hand, we have a party that has been compliant and complicit with this leftist/communist takeover of America (the Republican Party), and on the other, we have a party that treats us like pawns and helpless children (the Democratic Party). I believe that since we must choose in order to have a say and a political platform to be part of the decision-making as it relates to the policies of the land, we should choose the party that, in spite of their indifference to us, is more likely to create policies that support the free market and best align with biblical principles.

Faith.

Family.

Ownership.

The right to bear arms and defend yourself.

Smaller government.

Less regulation in business.

Lower taxes.

Freedom of speech.

These are conservative values, and though many Black families share them, we often vote against them, largely out of ignorance. This is primarily because the people who defend these values don't look like us, nor do they fully understand or recognize the unique struggles of our community. We allowed the media to associate our values with a "white racist" persona. What I've learned is that many of the people we label as racist share the same values, hopes, and dreams that we do and are far less concerned with race than we've been led to believe. We love to talk about Black Wall Street, highlighting the thriving communities of color, but we fail to recognize that these builders were freed slaves or the sons and daughters of slaves. They faced severe mistreatment, received no government assistance, held conservative values, and were Bible-believing Christians. They were unified, had strong families—most of which were two-parent homes—and called on the Lord for their help. Our modern-day deviation from these principles has been the largest contributor to the situation we find ourselves in today. Those who claim to care about our condition have either made it worse or exploited it for political gain.

I don't believe a vote for Trump will single-handedly bring sweeping change to our community, but I do think his policies could help create the conditions for us to facilitate that change ourselves. We have pledged our allegiance to the Democratic Party for decades with little to show for it, and yet we complain that Republicans aren't concerned about us. Why should they be, when we've collectively decided not to listen to them or even consider their policies? They stopped trying to appeal to us—why bother when there's no incentive?

This has led to a monopoly on the Black vote. When an entity faces no competition, it has no incentive to improve its service or act in the best interest of those it serves. I encourage those in my community to turn off mainstream media, listen to people who share your values but not your political views, do your research, and then make an informed decision. I have.

Follow Jesus.

www.ingramcontent.com/pod-product-compliance
Lightning Source LLC
Chambersburg PA
CBHW032122280326
41933CB00009B/952